Life Inside the Body

Life Inside the Body

Poems by

Susan Whitmore

© 2020 Susan Whitmore. All rights reserved.
This material may not be reproduced in any form, published,
reprinted, recorded, performed, broadcast,
rewritten or redistributed without
the explicit permission of Susan Whitmore.
All such actions are strictly prohibited by law.

Cover design by Shay Culligan

Cover photograph by Alexander Krivitskiy

ISBN: 978-1-952326-28-8

Kelsay Books
502 South 1040 East, A-119
American Fork, Utah, 84003

Acknowledgments

Poems in this manuscript previously appeared in the following literary journals and anthologies:

34th Parallel: "Egg, Ox, Ax," "The Fat Man and the She Bear"
Chance of a Ghost: "Greek Girls"
Crosscurrents: "The Priest"
The Furious Gazelle: "Hymn," "Lady Godiva Decides to Stay in Bed," "Seed"
Georgetown Review: "Rain"
Georgia Review: "Conception"
I-70 Review: "Away in the Manger," "Cricket," "Coda," "Communion," "Daffodil," "Lemons," "Life Inside the Body," "Season," "The Sorrow Tree"
Melusine: "Shore"
New Letters: "The Table"
Stone Highway Review: "Organ Music"
Touchstone: "Prince Myshkin"
Whirlybird Anthology of Kansas City Writers: "Cassandra at the Café"

Gratitude also to Write Club, a group of gifted Kansas City writers who read many of these poems in their beginning stages: Greg Field, Liz Gilbert, Teresa Keller Godsey, Joe Short, Ann Slegman Isenberg and Maryfrances Wagner.

Contents

Harbor	13
Still There Is This	14
Lion	15
Where You Are Now	16
Daffodil	18
Cricket	20
Season	21
The Glass Airplane	23
Lemons	25
Shore	27
Rain	28
Annunciation	29
The Table	30
Conception	32
Prince Myshkin	33
Organ Music	35
Away in the Manger	37
Hymn	39
Communion	41
The Priest	43
Throat Chakra Blue	44
Greek Girls	45
Eurydice in Headlights	46
Down	47
Cassandra at the Café	48
Clytemnestra	49
Persephone	50
The Bull	51
Egg, Ox, Ax	53
Seed	57
The Sorrow Tree	58
Key	59

Boat	60
Dreck and Music	61
Lady Godiva Decides to Stay in Bed	62
Life Inside the Body	63
The River	64
Coda	65
The Fat Man and the She Bear	66
The Altar	69

Harbor

Lost at sea, the ship's guy-wires sing.
Sails billow white toward sky, toward water.
Night is an eye wheeling blind into morning.

Teiresias places a squirming ewe on the stone,
Knows by intuition where to drive the knife,
Separate the white disks of bone into future.

Long after the animal mind leaves its altar,
The heart beats. The departing soul listens—
An ear opened on a sigh rising from the cradle.

Then silence—a hide hushed against its home.
Every sacrifice is a laugh and sob, wet
As blood despite dry wood's crack and kindle,

The sweet, red fire wed to the throb inside
The mountain overlooking the sea,
Waiting for the guy-wire's song in the harbor.

Still There Is This

When I get up, it's dark.
Sometimes the moon is sweeping

Like an eye over the planet
And there is frost on the window.
By the time I get to work

The eastern sky is golden
And I find myself reflected
In the black silhouette of trees.

But I am not a tree.
How does this happen,
What goes on in me?

The heard breath is mine,
But there are those trees standing,
Emblem of my longing.

The sun is rising and the trees
And I become light.
What part of the body is changed?

I know something changes—for
How my breath stops. And then quickens.

Lion

All day I've done no talking, my spine
A ladder of light. Still the question comes—

How long? You are not here, but I can taste
You in the gingko tree's fullness,

Afternoon sun angled low in the grass.
Each moment without you is blessed

In its purpose—to arrive and pass.
Who dares question what is destined?

Love is as thorough as a lion
Quartering its prey to get at the heart.

Where You Are Now

I

One hundred suns have been burning
For the hundred days since the one day that
Uncurled a fist to reveal your motionless heart.

The vivid beam of your body still rises
Like sap on fire along the steps of my spine,
Keeping me awake at night—

The length of your white thigh blazing.
Two delicate shoulder blades.
A breast illuminated against a pillow.

Five months, a superfluity of hours
On fire, grief rendered to an edgy acuity
I'd never have end. I will not bend.

II

At dawn, I leave the house and walk
Into another one of your unlived days
Flaunting itself in flamingo pink and tangerine

As the sun rises (one hundred and one)
Between the birches, brittle and bare of leaves—
Skeleton sentinels keeping vigil on the horizon

And cradling your bright in their branches.
Despite my maudlin pleading,
The sun won't quit. The birches keep standing.

And here is my own breath, composing
For the thousandth time its song of love—
My inevitable heart. Still beating.

Daffodil

Welcome adversity as a pleasant surprise.
Prize calamity as your own body.
                                    —*Lao Tzu*

I

Porch chimes ring though the open window
On air smelling both spring and winter,
Daffodils bending low under frost after three
Warm days' joy. The candle flame flickers
In the breeze I breathe in, ears tuned to pine
Needle branches brushing against each other.

I know a story about change, how change
Wears the face of loss. Loss has buried my face
Under covers at night, rendering the beloved
Bed a sky of stars and black—nothing to grip
Without being burned or thrust far into past.
Everything seen and felt is real. Time is spiral.

II

Each moment's impression sparks the senses.
Daffodils turn to sun one day, then give up
Their gold to new-green loam. Don't despair:
The bulb holds life despite the flower's failure.
Every spring sports daffodils, more than we
Can grasp or gather with two hands, two eyes.

Grief makes us larger. I'm grateful for sorrow:
The spirit now rises to better occasion,
The body to greater gift, a plethora of daffodils
Held intact as a hard, round promise in the ground—
No matter how life is profoundly transfigured.
Here on the planet we are loved. We are loved.

Cricket

The crickets sound sweet after the season's turn,
Myriad insect souls intersecting with my own.
I'd like to be counted among the most basic,

Critical as the individual cricket or clematis just now
Calling it a day, now that the hyacinth and crocus
That slept through winter are roused by spring.

Life is calling, even as evening calls forth our undoing,
Every childhood terror now become blessing—
My mother's eight-year illness has versed me well

In how to die. I am no longer afraid at her passing.
The crickets humming through the open window
Trill toward coupling. The tulips in the garden

Are pregnant with petals. I'm dreaming,
Lately, the white hand of snow falling gentle
On bare birch, its limbs pristine and austere

Against a gray winter sky. I'm dreaming crisp depletion
While the heart my mother made beats warmly
Against my ribcage, a red moon caught between

Boughs of bone. This is the sonata of gain and loss,
Two seasons sounding simultaneously, that I might best
Hold what thrives and fails without discrimination—

My mother's whole life held open like a mouth.
I will drink it down without compromise.

Season

I

Sweetness rolls down, a bright ball bearing
Singing nonsense, a brain-dead cell
That can't think a single thing, a divine idiot,

A ghost lobbied over to the other side—
Into light. This body doesn't know what
To do with itself, the body no longer able to hold

Onto substance. Still, sweetness spills down,
A ball bearing rolling through the broken engine—
No purpose but to roll and shine and flare.

II

My mother did not turn her face away. Harmony
Arrived, despite mistakes and the broken angles
Of plans—all her strategies crumbled in a heap.

I used to keep an eye open even in sleep,
An ear open for the angels calling her home.
Now there is laughter in the sick room—

No shame, no shame. It only remains
For my mother to rise, a bent-legged foal
Stumbling toward the ecstasy of pasture.

III

She will lower her muzzle to ground,
Tongue wet grass, let her limbs fold into perfect
Posture—no stress; no striving. She has known

This soil before. She has known this sky and rain.
When the body becomes one with earth again,
The redwings wake and sing. Phlox spreads

A blue root. I know the name for this:
Sweetness. Love is enough. Spring is enough.
Season of juniper, burgeoning with new berries.

The Glass Airplane

We're all flying in the same glass airplane,
Despite disparate countries. Notwithstanding
Our walls of mortar and brick, a single, open eye

Sees through turbulent weather and worry.
Nothing distinguishes us from atmosphere—
The earth we think close is miles below our feet.

One moon rises white over undulating terrain.
My exhaled breath is your inward, two notes
Of the same song. This much we wish for—

To go on living, to love, to know we are loved.
Discord breeds harmony when sorrow is held
Long enough to become singing in minor key,

An ear open on the meter of what exists
Coda after coda, free-falling toward ground,
Like an engine slipping its grip and stalling

Until gears finally hit home and the plane
Levels out between the thunderhead chorus.
When someone asks for your coat, say *Yes.*

When someone's arms are empty, fill their arms
With your body. If you have no coat, ask another
For their coat. If your arms are empty, open

Your arms like the wings of the anhinga and wait.
When someone weeps, cry also. The betrayal
Keeping a wound fresh in your billowing heart—

Smother it with kisses. Cover your transgressor
With kisses. Don't ask questions of foreign language,
Speak a third dialect that never gets tangled

Between tongues. The glass airplane will land
Without a crack in the country of the beloved,
Where all bodies remain unbroken and bright.

Lemons

It is out of the abundance of the heart that the mouth speaks.
Luke 6:45

I

No bad tree bears good fruit, the Gospel says.
But in Naples, I saw the worst lemon tree ever,
The shadow of a lemon tree stricken by sunlight—

No reason for the withered limbs, stick trunk,
Leaves more brown than green and brittle as paper.
You'd think the tree dead but for its incandescent

Lemons—a hundred brights loading thin branches
Down to breaking, the fruit having sucked all wet
Out of the wood, because wet is what lemons need.

There stood tart, yellow-white abundance,
Life shining like sin on a dissipated tree ready
To lose its grip on ground, so great was joy's weight.

II

No bad tree bears good fruit, the Gospel says.
But in my own Kansas City I've seen a man give
His last-gotten coin to the next man in need,

A fat lemon passed from palm to palm on a street
Strewn with blowing litter, boon blossoming
Out of a bad place. Better to give everything away

In winter, trust the sun to give back a hundred-fold
Harvest come spring, a gift so heavy one's arm
Strain under the burden of gift. The fruit we bear

Drops back to ground no matter how the body
Is nurtured—the stuff of profit, the stuff of dreams.
This is the way of lemons, the way of all food.

Shore

Lust is an illiterate organ beating its pulse
Against the ground, a feathered wing past thought,
Speaking, or writing it down. Lust has no reason.

Water grinds salty teeth against the beach,
A white tongue licking sand. Gulls fly overhead,
Dropping black pits from the plums I've thrown,

Purple fists clasped neat around each seed.
Here's a firm hand on the thigh, blue Atlantic
Thrumming an ode on the clavicle's chord—

We didn't know you could sing, the clouds say.
The hand is a brush stroke opening a throat
On Botticelli, fat Cupids with dimpled bottoms

Flitting about a woman grown slack after love.
The whole landscape—pastoral sheep, silver
Cottonwoods, the dumbfounded shepherd—

All held between her quivering knees. Here's
Flesh cradled in the palm's need, wet plum pits
Stripped of their sweet and gathering sand.

Now the gulls' satisfaction sounds distant above
The cypress-lined shore, a song disappearing
Into the body's dissipation, these breaking waves.

Rain

Delectable aperture, drop and pour
Into the bedeviled places I've lost
Accounting for—washed away, lucid water.

Communication's letters and numbers
Fall apart, the tethered lexicon I thought
Would hold the body's boat together

Frayed at the cleat. The cargo carefully packed
Cracks in the bow. I fear secrets spilling,
A roster undone, many papered lists

Projected for naught. Now wind fills the sail
With a substance I cannot see, a fine thing
Strong as faith that moves the boat

Toward the shore while the rain falls
Against the white and blue. No secrets,
No spooks hidden in the helioscope's hinge,

No codes to crack or map to decipher the journey
Home. A simple story is all. Each droplet
On the lake is a tiny open mouth singing.

Annunciation

There was a wound left to heal, despite tales
Of intact virginity. Gabriel's not the soft bird
You'd imagine, but a conflagration of wings
That won't take no for an answer. Jesus came

Honest to his single denial—I was first to say,
Take this cup from me, its content of baby,
Blood, and sacrifice—my own love lost in
Ascension, all souls who cared to drink, saved.

Our last night, Joseph and I walked the market
Under the heads of strung up chickens and goats,
Fresh green olives and figs perfect as testicles
Cradled in our fists. My father approved of Joseph,

Dimmed the lanterns late at night, all the while
Knowing we talked together under the stable's eve
Among sleeping sheep. We were to settle in Egypt,
No thought of Galilee or God-forsaken Jerusalem

Where people palm silver like spirit. Those days,
The stars were no more course to salvation than
My beloved's touch on the skin of our future home.
The Gospel leaves out the rotten night I spent

After, how poppies turned black, moon blinking
Shut on our plans. Soon enough Joseph divined
My loins growing hot under that strange seed,
A new map for travel emblazoned on his fingers.

Think of this when you pray at my feet for comfort—
The night our Savior took on life in ironic shroud
I wanted to break my own womb from its body.
My beloved made vassal—and me, the vessel.

The Table

St. Joseph's Day

Joseph must have been Sicilian, won his Mary over
With pasta frolla and zuccotto con amaretti after coffee
While blue drained the Mediterranean and the moon

Lay its white head on water. Breakfast, he'd show up
At her house bearing frutta brinata in a basket, succulent
Figs from his father's orchard, a jug of sweet wine

Cool stone cellar fermented and corked with calf skin.
Joseph's courtship paints Mary's lips chiacchiere
And kisses, thighs and breasts spreading honey and gold,

Blond soufflé al formaggio belly swelling her
Robin's egg robe so elegantly, the angels take notice
And Gabriel makes his visit. On Annunciation Day

Joseph's in the kitchen splitting a tuna open,
Pulls the delicate skeleton intact from wet pink flesh
Prior to stuffing with mousse ai funghi (the loamy

Mushrooms he'd found under eucalyptus leaves);
And Mary's beneath the grape arbor, licking brine
From firm green olives her suitor cured in wooden cask—

Until the child arrives, she'll swear it was the pit
She swallowed, eating with too much eagerness, tart fruit
Cracking in her teeth, no thought but for the next.

Joseph says the guy who knocked her up will die
By the knife he uses to decapitate chickens, calls Mary
Madonne chooch, has his day of cursing all the angels.

Then he chooses to believe her. And then he chooses to accept.
Although it was only Mary he wanted to feed, surely
There's enough spaghetti Milanese—and sweet—for three.

Conception

There's pasta carbonara in bed long after the lights
Go out in the rooms of the house—we eat bacon, egg,
Fettuccine sweaty and sexy, sucking on the rind

Of the grated lemon, aged Parmesan, and suddenly
There's hunger again for that white Cape Cod house
Seen from the other side of Beaver Lake, its windows

Lit at dusk like golden eyes, sight sprinkled into ribbons
Across the water more yellow than the bright trail
Of moonlight, and I'm sitting there with my brothers

At the table in summer night heat in the screen porch
By lantern playing gin rummy and drinking Black Label
As the eels begin to surface on the lake with their scaled

And pointed heads, and again my first lover lays me down
In Yundt's lily field, saying, *Don't expect music or violins,*
And I'm raising a flute to my lips as the space in Franck's

Symphonie en D falls open for me and the whole orchestra
Waits while my little sister holds her baby Andrea,
Swinging the rag doll by its worn neck like the pendulum

In the sleepy grandfather clock in Dr. N's waiting room
Where I wait until finally my unborn Robert runs me through
Amsterdam rain before breaking me in two and gluing me

Back together as I lie on the white, red, white Venray
Hospital bed. He comes to me with open mouth, closed fists,
Fighting, powerless and angry, bloody and not to blame.

Prince Myshkin

After Dostoyevsky's The Idiot

In the fog of your anxiety you step delicately—
The falling sickness is waiting in the wings,
On the edges of things. You step gently,
Acutely aware of the street you tread on,
The soft click of heels, one after the other,

The breeze on your temple that moves your hair.
And then—the moment of confusion when
All your disparate selves barrel through heart
And brain. You see yourself and flush with fear,
Concentrate quickly on what is in front of you—

On this day

It's a store window fronting a display
Of knives—a display of kitchen knives,
Swiss Army knives, some knives complete
In their own sheaths. You think, hard,
About knives—and as you take the shaky breath

That tells you this time you staved it off,
The sun comes out from behind clouds, dazzling
Pinwheels of light bring the glass to life,
And you see your shadow, your perfect shadow
Outlined on the window and looking in.

Turning back to the street

You are amazed at how everything has become
So something again with the sun's shining—
The red cobbled street, a fruit vendor in an apron
Palming plums, a woman in a fur-lined hat clutching
A package to her chest and meeting your gaze.

It's all so real and clear, you laugh with relief—
How it exists! And when you begin to walk now
It's no longer softly. You step easy and with weight,
Sure-footed like someone in new boots measuring
And treading the land he knows belongs to him.

Organ Music

I

The vibrating lungs of Rheims billow out to God:
Vast, dank walls wet like pleurisy or pneumonia
Illuminated by purple light penetrating stained glass.

I think I see my father place a white candle
Among a hundred flames in Mary's sequestered corner
Where folks pray for their dead or loved ones

Still sweating life out on pillows. The votive
In its wax-splattered home, he kneels at the rail
And places his face in a ten-fingered temple.

Mary says something I never can hear,
But my father raises his cataract-clouded eyes,
Meets her blue-painted iris gaze and smiles.

I'm hoping the candle is for me, as good as dead
After a decade of anger—how I told him once
He'd never again hold me or lift me from fear.

II

When I was six, my father took me
Into a heart housed in the Franklin Institute,
The organ big as a room with ventricled windows

Slamming shutters closed and open
To let museum guests through—rhythmic
As the real thing but decibels higher.

We walked pink arteries in black-blood light
Holding hands, not daring to touch the viscous,
Muscled walls. I'd known the heart to be fist-sized,

But impossibly huge fingers now closed
Over air and ground, squeezing me like a nut
Until my own heart unfurled its grip—my life

Let out at a tempo beyond the big heart's beat.
I cracked. My father carried me, crying,
Out the aorta into the bright brain of the museum.

III

It's not my father at the altar after all,
Or a candle lit for me, though surely each prayer
Is for all of us as the cathedral heart

Is all our hearts sounding—at least until
The body's door closes, and everything stops.
The Frenchman finishes praying,

Amen a kiss on the Virgin's alabaster toes.
I want to ask him to carry me, crying, out
And over the cobblestones, away from Rheims.

Another beat, and I see my father filling a feeder
With pinon nuts and sunflower seeds
On the lawn of our home outside Philadelphia.

I sink to my knees, the constricted fist
Inside me as still as the soaring stone arches
Promising forgiveness, up there in the dark.

Away in the Manger

I

Any woman with a seed unexpected inside her
Eventually finds herself in a stable, warmed
By animals keeping no truck with the attitudes
Of men. Faith is kept best at night by pressing
Close to each other. Insight weighs as much as
An unasked-for child given us to hold and carry,
See through to our death. Sacrifice is the boon
Sucked up to, whatever the fear, a last ember
Glowing in the grate with a heart sure enough
To set the whole body blazing again when
Breath rises just right—or wrong—

You choose the word and the way to say it—
To see it, the way to feel it as the limbs fold.

II

Every morning and birth are hope's resurrection,
Frost sparkling light on the grass and sunlit
Window, voice rising in a cloud to prove
Inside heat keeps kicking up its perfect spark.
Today the family's intact—tomorrow, in pieces.
Someone's left, or died—the father or mother
Who nursed children beyond her own obstacles.
Or it's you who's succumbed to accident, desire
Or disease. Perhaps today a child is conceived
With no name, born to a new life transforming
What we've come to plan for, wish, expect—

You choose the terror and how to deal with it—
Drink it under, sleep on it, embrace or let it go.

III

But think of the dumb, sweet animals,
Those who turn their heads to water without
Question. The mule after pulling the plough,
Butting goats come evening, sheep with their teeth
On succulent grass. Think of a calf falling wet
From the heifer who's found a shaded spot
At the field's edge to drop her shining burden,
The heifer bending to clear the small nose and mouth
With her tongue. Think of the dog and cat
Sleeping warm, one curled against the other
When the night is cold and even when it's not.

Do birds think, shall I not, or shall I, sing?
Does your heart's cadence choose its beat, silence, beat?

Hymn

The humming, of course, is not only in the ear.
It's your whole body.
                             —Li-Young Lee

I thought it best to pray since I was pregnant.
I sat in the cathedral's candle-lit corner
While flagrant sunset washed the field of leeks
Split by the River Maas blue and orange, dusk
After dusk, the whole spring I lived in Holland.

I thought it best to pray since I was pregnant,
As I thought it good to walk, to be careful
With wine, to be cautious of the wayward will
Kicking inside me—not the child's, but mine.
The cathedral was always empty at that hour

But for one old man rocking at the altar
Under a pressing need I could not know.
I sat in the back corner, not wanting to intrude,
But quitting my own prayer often to watch
The grief and rapture that drove him—

No acceptance in his bent knees, the bowed back,
His wool jacket steaming with humidity
From farm and fields. Whatever had gone wrong
Or lost that winter gripped him still that spring
Over the stretch of each evening, after the horses

Had been fed their oats and shut in the stable.
The sorrow he could not yet bear go home to
Weighed solid on his trembling shoulders,
His face buried in the rough sheets of his hands.
He never saw me, the pregnant woman

Wrapped in a wool sweater with mud on her boots
Sitting at the back of the cathedral's savory blue.
But we were a small family: The grief-stricken man,
The waiting child and me. Not one of us ever had
An answer, though the questions were endless.

Communion

After William Henry Lewis

The violin my daughter holds in her throat
Sings at ducks rippling Loose Park's lake,
An offering of bread swimming them to her

With wide-open beaks, a note inside each.
The feathered crowd gains the bank, placing
Webbed feet alongside her sandals' dance.

Devout as a priestess bestowing body on
Congregation, she sets her jaw on purpose
Not separate from God, the small hands

That will be woman extended to let food
Fall into music. The wind lifts her hair
Until the scalp shines through—and I'm back

Under Little Charlie's guitar arc, beat
The boon out of Grand Emporium to manna
Swirling in the gyre that keeps the planet

Spinning. Bliss opens hands on heaven,
Now on me, touch a wafer dissolving want
On the tongue, a sip of wine sweetened deep

By sacrifice: *All those nights I wasn't dancing.*
My daughter, almost three, raises her palms
On similar rhythmic need—leaves grooving

Free of the linden's grip, winter's breath
Etched in hieroglyph across the window,
A symphony of intricate, glistening filament

With a translucent spider conducting at center—
Or now, the ring of white down settling
Slow-song about her, once the bread is gone.

The Priest

He writes his sermon by candlelight,
Smoking hand-rolled cigarettes
And stripped to his shorts by the fire,
Loving despite promise the self he strokes.

The priest knows he holds his people
Between his lips, a flagrant, unremitting desire
On his tongue no matter what he preaches—
Nails through palms, the harlot's hair

Falling over the wet feet of Jesus,
One fish and loaf split to feed five hundred,
Blue carp sliding through the Apostles' fingers
As they witness the peerless walk on water.

God in all of it, and the Devil in God
Offering up his choice and chalice.
On Sunday, sin films the priest's cheeks.
More than listen, the gathered watch him,

Warm and adoring as when he wakes
With the sun on his face. True love
Was unexpected. He's thinking—
I've been sleeping—What is more holy

Than the moist underworld rising
To shine on a woman's brow as she strains
New life into existence? Little did he know
The power of the assembled congregation,

All eyes on him as he proclaims the Word
Of God, a Peter admitting three times
Over the need he's come to know
In his soul—because he wants to live.

Throat Chakra Blue

It's impossible to stutter when you sing.
              —Megan Washington

My avatar is active, doppelganger masquerade
What I think—say—feel sequined up into glitter
A word strip tease born of root-chakra red

It's not my policy to forget about my face
But I've burned down to spleen, spleen seeds
Scattering—one truth two truth three truth

Vowels climb the spine ladder one bright bone
At a time—A E I O U—a conflagration of
Consonants—S R T B Q—my third eye siren

Wailing—I am trying on my avatar clothes
Pulling on motorcycle boots, zipping up
A leather jacket, slipping jangly plastic bangles

On my wrists, I am trying on my avatar body
Wagging a second tongue, swallowing
In another throat, squaring up my hips

Bending at the knees. She has things to say
That may or may not benefit me, but
No matter, throat-chakra blue won't wait

Greek Girls

Iphigenia's father spills her blood into the Aegean
And then Cassandra loses life to his wife's butcher knife.
Daphne's refuge from rape is the laurel tree's trunk.
Io's, to be cow, bending knees on muddy ground.

Leda can't write, her hands are white-tipped wings.
Dido drowns in surf, incomplete without Aeneas.
Ariadne strangles herself with Theseus' thread.
Helen of Troy gives beauty a nasty name.

Hera grows fat on green jealousy and vengeance.
Philomela's tongue is cut out, lest she speak
Her hymen broken by her sister's husband.
Eurydice's lost to Hades after Orpheus' need to watch.

Persephone's a pawn to get the seasons going.
Pandora's inquisitive mind dooms all mankind.
Psyche burns for wanting it with the lights on.
Circe's scary because she knows when pigs are pigs.

Calypso's left weeping for loving Odysseus well.
The Sirens sing a salty song of seduction.
The Harpies raise well-honed claws.
Scylla and Charybdis open their devouring maws.

Medea, betrayed, rises to slaughter her sons.
Athena takes on the sword-stance of a man.
Only Sappho, chewing on the honeyed hyacinth,
Says *Damn I don't think so* and sets word to stone.

Eurydice in Headlights

Rural Route 2

ICU's blue light falls on Orpheus' shoulders,
Illuminating his skin like Aegean sand on green sheets,
A handful of salt washed in the waves of his lover's tongue.

His wounds dry into strings of kelp after high tide,
A brown-stitched filigree strung across his sleeping back
Relaxed as a lute caved in on itself. Orpheus dreams

His lung's instrument song keeps Eurydice complete
And seated on the motorcycle, thighs wrapped tight
Around his hips—dreams her rising from the ghost-hawk

Florescent juniper she flew into, honing in on prey
Only she could see between berries and root—
Dreams her rising now with skull intact. Better than

Their own fate, Orpheus drives Eurydice along the route,
Not looking back for the second it takes to lose grip
On the gas, send a bike skidding. Despite triple-headed

Cerberus' barking, a single note remains whole
In Orpheus' throat as he keeps his gaze steady on
The dog's eye yellow line guiding them both home.

Down

Leda loved swans until one bit her, leaving a wound
She would not forget. At the river's edge,
He held her hair in his mouth and pulled her under.

Leda filled her fists with bluegrass from the bank.
There was a flurry of down. Then, for years,
Sand-bottom silt under her nails, mud between her teeth,

And feathers floating about her in dreams—sharp
In their tips and soft as skin elsewhere, confusing her
Endlessly. Leda never quite regained her balance.

When she grew old and tangled, she was always
Leaning so far to one side or the other we were sure
She was about to fall, bloody her knees and elbows

Like a child. Of course, she had no choice in the matter.
I can't speak for the boys, but the girls I know,
The girls grow up to call it sacrifice, a special gift—

The one thing they're good at. We call it art, the swan's
Commanding, white wings and brilliant, open beak
Committed to the end, as if monogamy was an answer.

Cassandra at the Café

Cassandra's at the bar forgetting Agamemnon,

No thought of the blue Aegean or the last sheep
Letting its throat go like red wine on the stone.
One sip and her teeth freeze in bas-relief against

Her tongue, saline as an oyster hiding its pearl,
What she knows bypassing domestic trouble
Easy as water over the mind's stubborn altar.

Foreknowledge is a tendoned hand binding
The sacrificial body to a reality she'd wash away
In libations of tequila and scotch, flushing

Wild animal fear from the animated brain
That despite intention names moment and loss—
Brass tacks of memory nailing her prophetic palms

To a cross that stands straight in muddy ground
She doesn't think able to hold root or voice future.
Who wouldn't choose cool comfort, past and present

Nested finally quiet in the heart? Cassandra
Would rather live in denial, drink the fisted grip
Of imminent fate down until the blessed entrails

Are ordered for good on the unbiased pillar
Of her spine, the sapling meant for kindling
Moist enough to keep its green and thwart fire.

Clytemnestra

Clytemnestra is no Penelope.

You can bet she doesn't pass her nights at the loom,
Listening to doves mating under the eaves of the home
Her husband abandons for war over another woman—
That Helen, launching ships from as far away as
Argos and Crete to bring her back to rightful bed.

It's a guy thing, Agamemnon says, packing his bags
Along with the best twenty pigs from the stable,
Get with the program. Never one for platitudes,
Clytemnestra takes the first suitor who can pronounce
Her name correctly, trades her promise for sex

After grief over Iphigenia, her daughter's cry
Sounding all the way from the Aegean's inverted
Blue eye to the House of Atreus, lodging rage
In Clytemnestra's black liver and magenta spleen.
Waiting never makes what's crooked straight

Or the back-door approach of Medea who slit
Her children's throats at Jason's betrayal.
Clytemnestra takes her cue from the hawk and flies
Directly to the rodent heart, trades her love for justice
And slides a blade into her husband's homecoming.

Persephone

The sound of cottonwoods moving in wind, the air
Full of flying leaves, and these cows—stable, watching—
Knowing what Demeter's daughter is too frenetic to grasp.

Persephone twirls with white-fluffed seeds as they circle
And swirl. The fields lie soft over earth's strong muscle,
Sable rolling over darker flesh and moaning more deeply

Than the trees' roar, the wind's cry, the bovine lowing.
Above all, the wide and quiet bowl of sky—a blue eye
Hazed with dust the farmer's plough kicks over and up.

The grass moves in tongues, the cottonwoods creak,
Silver leaves catch low light and sing about their burning.
Persephone is melodramatic, moved. But this is real—

She wants her beloved's hands in her hair, his mouth
On her throat. There is love in this bending of limbs
To ground, the airborne seed bound for bed in eager earth.

The Bull

I

Ariadne slaps bare soles across the stones of Crete
Alongside waves breaking like afterbirth
On the shore she's finally grown enough to reach.

The spiral of string wound about her sweaty fingers
Mirrors the DNA of procreation, blasting
Her father in the face of such magnificent genes—

Theseus unafraid in the Minotaur's maze, hunting
The beast beneath skin. Ariadne knows any man
Strong enough to dare becomes what he kills—

Theseus is just the sort to love her, to take
A bull-horn thrust into the soft of his palms.
Throughout her youth the sanguine animal

Frothed at the mouth outside her window,
His velvet hide cradled on her tongue each night
While the clatter of hooves rang in her ears.

II

The length a woman in love will go to equals
A skein of silk spun from the guts of a worm,
Or the shift—worn since childhood—unraveling

Recurring dreams of salt and waves building
On the blue Aegean's horizon, snarled in a way
The wayward mind can't reach. Ariadne holds fast

To one end of the thread, throws its length
Like a lasso around her beloved's neck,
Drawing him out of the labyrinth into white light,

Her body a land any weary warrior would relish.
We all know Theseus wouldn't have made it alone.
The length a man in love will go to equals

Confusion's shadowed walls dazzled by bellows,
No thought given to the way out until
The Minotaur heart spills its blood on stone.

III

Two lovers: Each thinks the other a savior.
Each grip tightly their end of the string binding
The knot around the throat of the third between:

The brilliant brute they can't live with or without.
Why else does one cry out in joy when grasping
Has reached its peak and breaks on open air,

The exhaled breath of the wave's crest dissipating
Into sand? Theseus follows the thread back
To Ariadne's hand, but his swig of relief is brief

As gratitude giving way to the next necessity.
After a month of sex warm as the bull's entrails
Spread on the altar of sacrifice and atonement

Theseus leaves her—the string meant for salvation
Coiled inextricably about Ariadne's neck,
An indecipherable future tangled in her fingers.

Egg, Ox, Ax

I. Potential Chicken

An egg sits in a cardboard carton
Nestled in with another eleven,
Sits among eleven brothers and sisters
And listens. Is the egg a chicken?
Does the egg have an ear?
No, you can count the reasons—
The egg has no feathers, no beak, no wings.
No visible ear. Plucked from the warm ass
Of its mother into cold storage, the egg
Lost its chickenhood. An egg unfertilized—
At best, only half a potential chicken.

The unfertilized half a potential chicken
Turns up a yellow eye in the skillet.
Was the chicken spirit ever there
In the egg—to be, and go?
Probably not, but you don't know.
What you know is that the egg now grows
White and gold in sputtering butter.
First the crack and food thereafter—
Gift of the mother chicken body,
Gift of larger spirit outside the hen
That meant to make another bird.
Which is not, in fact, what has come to pass.
You have an egg for breakfast instead.

When did your spirit arrive?
Was it in your mother's womb,
Your eyes open in the sixth month
When you could see light shining
Through bloody veins and viscera?
Or do you remember your half-self,

The egg you were once, settled in ovary
Before hormones and love set you traveling
Down the dun tunnel toward existence?
I'm not saying *Don't eat eggs.* I'm just saying
Think about the perfect chicken strutting
In yesterday's farmyard. And you now,
A great big body, bending to gather an egg.

II. Ignorant Ox

It may be true—the more savory
The morsel, the more spirit meat once had.
Consider bacon, crisp fat edging
The tang of salty, ribboned meat at center,
Sizzling alongside the now stagnant
Lump of egg on your plate.
How much livelier the bacon!
And isn't it the bacon that lingers
On your tongue, asking you for a drink
Of water to set your constitution right
Two hours after breakfast? That's the pig
Singing in you, the same pig that raised
Its head for the blow at the butchering
Now kicking up its hooves in you.

I'm not saying *Don't eat bacon.* I'm just saying
A dance goes on in the body after you've eaten,
After the perfect pig is disseminated
In your mouth and gullet. Pig gift.
Succulent bacon popping in the pan,
Melting then on your tongue, so luscious
You could bend a knee in thanksgiving.
Here's fertilization complete—

Loin of the pig that once suckled its mother's teat
And found a place amid muck
Before finally finding a seat your table.

In ancient Greece, a priest leads an ox
To the altar, where grain ripened by sun
Lies consecrated on the stone. The ox,
Knowing what it loves—which is another way
Of saying *Knowing what it needs*—eats the grain.
But it is sacrilege to eat grain consecrated into God.
By law, the offending animal must be killed.
The priest bares the beast's throat and spills
Blood by ax onto the same stone. The ox meat
Profaned by eating and made sacred by grain
Is roasted and offered to the ritual's initiates—
You and me, sitting down to breakfast.

III. The Ax

If consecrated grain is enough to condemn
The ox, then the ox, having eaten the grain,
Is also God. What then of the priest
Who raised the ax against divine bellows
To spill God's blood on the altar stone?
If the ox must die, why not the priest?
The ritual proceeds in ancient Greece—
The robed elder enacting holy edict
Cannot be held accountable, so the ax
Is tried in divinity's court, found guilty
And cast out to sea amid incantations.
We get to eat and the priest goes free.

Dare you doubt your divinity?
One day the flesh you love and nurture
Will return to feed the boll weevil and corn,
To the earth entrusted with the enormous oak
That stands to sweep wide, wooden arms
On sky and drop acorns for skirmishing
Squirrels. The squirrels feed
On the fruit of the tree, a bit of you,
A bit of me, a bit of God—
That they might live to see the blossoming,
Impossible, inevitable spring.

A lot to contemplate over breakfast.
We of the wet and open, deserving mouth.
Honor the egg, the potential but not to be chicken,
The pig, the ignorant ox, the priest,
The ax cast out to sea against transgression.

Seed

After Edward Weston

Embers whisper crisply now the blaze is gone,
Extolling statuary among a ruined temple's pillars.
The enigmatic Pythia lisps a prophecy in tongues

While shrouded crows shuffle black cloud incantation
In branches, spreading and stretching night-time wings,
Excited in the silent, still cypress—but staying put.

If I dream right tonight, I'll wake later to insight,
My body and brain cracked open, a pinecone on fire,
One Pythian syllable settled like a seed in my throat.

The Sorrow Tree

My sorrow tree is laden with leaves black as soot
But its fruit is sweet and red. I eat until I'm sick.
My helpless reverence for you makes this necessary.

Far more than any kindness, your wrong made you
An intimate. Your wrong is a bird that won't stop
Cracking seeds in the cage of my breast.

I have tried to walk out of the skin I'm in.
I moved to another place with trees
Laden with leaves green as a hurricane.

But their fruit was brown and bitter.
Of course, I crawled back into the branches of
My sorrow tree and set up house.

No one can make me move. No one can move me.
You are as gone as yesterday's breath, gone as the sun
That set two weeks ago. Last year's rain on the lake

Drank you up and spread you into its billion other
Drops of water. I can't recall your face.
But I remember how you tasted. Sweet as an apple.

Key

After Jorge Luis Borges

Ten years ago, quite by accident,
I saw you stepping out of a shower.
You slid free of the stippled glass
Into crisp, naked clarity
Draped in a swirl of steam and lavender.

A slice of sunshine lit up one brilliant thigh.
Everyone else turned their heads.

Today you don't remember. Ten years
And you have not thought of it once.
But the moment took root in me as
A recurring dream that cracks my sleep
Every time I enter sorrow's dun tunnel.

Today I'm telling you the story over coffee.
A wet snow blankets the cobblestones outside.

I say,

The little key that opens a house to us
Is a memory of you ten years ago
When I saw you stepping out of a shower
And the lock set fast in me suddenly slipped free
And all my doors and windows blew open.

Boat

I would like not minding, whatever travels my heart.
         —Jane Hirschfield

Darling, I know it is not your love
Which makes me free or your distance a prison.

The still eye at the hurricane's center is
The only spot inside emotion entirely
Disconnected and unmoved by anything—

Pine planks from the dock, white sails loosened
From their rigging, a skipper's hat, feathers
From the herring gull. And here we are now

In stormy seas. Here I am in the boat that keeps
Sinking, this boat I keep patching with promise
And prayer. One would think despair a good teacher—

But no, I only come to love the boat more each time
It sinks under the weight of feeling. And no,
It's not love, but that sickness, an attachment

To too much sugar or salt: One makes one fat,
The other, too thin. Obesity and emaciation.
So no, it's not love, but a boat sickness.

Dreck and Music

It's the memory of how I loved him—
The forever-promise giving way
To another need as the furniture trembled
And the hallways narrowed, the electric wires
Behind drywall tangling like hair,

Humming betrayal. My married house
Was filled with light when I entered
And dark with smoke when I left.
Everything changes.
It's the memory of how I loved him—

How I love him still only more finely
Now I don't need him. My daughter
Opened her mouth like a bird on the day
She was born and sang notes the rivers
Know how to sing—the constancy of love,

What rises above the dreck of a broken home—
The cracked crystal, a thermometer's mercury
Running loose in the sink and freed of fever,
An asbestos cloud released after years
From its wallpaper layers, a door

Swung open forever—like the promise
Dangling now in sunlight, moonlight,
Sunlight between the strands
Of my daughter's hair. How gentle
The white scalp, the sweet skull just beneath.

Lady Godiva Decides to Stay in Bed

We've all been spat on the earth,
Coughed up to clear the throat
Of an enormous machine I cannot fathom.

I'd work at it, learn which levers to pull,
Get grimy and greasy, read a manual—
If I'd get paid for my time.

But the company is broke, declared
Bankruptcy years ago, and no one
Is home at the Union. There's nowhere

To turn my Green Stamps in these days.
It was a quaint idea, anyway—as if
An umbrella might shelter me from hurt,

Or a camera, help me see the world's colors
Right. Saving speaks of fathers long dead,
Miscellaneous drawers cluttered with

Wooden clothespins and extra keys
No one can remember what for anymore,
Pieces of string too short to bind anything.

Now we pay our bills with cash—
That many checks have buoyed and bounced.
The children yearn with open mouths.

Riding horses won't change the tax levied
On a woman's skin, the way the body
Is eaten by life when one chooses the usual.

Life Inside the Body

I like the way my boots fit,
Finally, after two winters of wear,
And the sound of my heels on wood.

I like the way my hip sockets swivel
Perfectly in the pelvic bone, smooth
As silver, as I walk down the hallway.

I live alone inside my body, a blue flame
Glued to shining sinew and tendon,
Woven into the web of skin

That keeps the lifeboat skimming
The bright water of this day, that.
I would that you could touch me

There, but it's not the way it works.
Apparently. And I've tried.
There was the time you found me

Weeping on your doorstep,
Making a mess of the flagstones.
And all those nights I tangled

My fingers in your hair, trying
To pull you inside. Turns out, pleasure
Can be had in boots, swinging

My own hips in the hallway,
The miracle of skeletal construction
As tangible as desire.

The River

After Colum McCann

Desire is a horse knowing well how to work—
Shoulder the harness, split earth without
The whip's instigation, eager to please the God
That keeps the stable warm. All animals pray

In a slow-tongued way for an end to thirst.
Who would guess salvation's wet exacts a cost
Indifferent as the weather, seizing what it wants
Without ethic? Or that the work-horse neck bent

To water invites disaster, one foot in the shallows
Long before the river starts to rise? Desire
Would see, if desire was wise, the clouded sky
So thick with rain, dirt from the field rises in it.

Rocks hidden in the muddy stream that snare
The hoof won't move until the current kisses
The wild, upturned eyes, flooding the seeded acre
And lifting the stable from its stone foundation.

Coda

Beethoven's Symphonie en C minor

After the peopled extravaganza and an abundance
Of serial monogamy couched in sweet melodrama, silence
Bangs a mallet against the dull drum of the house.

I am wandering in my palms and the soles of my feet.
I am wandering through rooms. I am considering
The conundrum of you and the love-hate continuum.

Somewhere far away you are breathing.
Somewhere far away there is a light slivered under your door.
The quiet between notes is deafening.

I don't expect the next phrase to come,
When there you are again in pre-dawn birds' clipped singing,
Quietly at first, then cacophony and demand—

The insistent conductor driving the strings on
With the whip of his baton until all the instruments
Must run home to the coda, coda, coda and close.

The Fat Man and the She Bear

I

The fat man has left his alabaster throne
To sit on a circle of warm fur: The she-bear
He shot last winter on the Canadian crack

Of the Continental Divide, when he was snow-shoe thin.
Now he peels new potatoes still caked with dirt,
Because it pleases him—his fingers and knuckles

Numb with brown water. *Oh, sweet baby—*
He's dreaming, peeling—*How your claws
Are like moon-stone jewels, how the heat*

*And pressure of your glass gaze emblazons me,
How bright your ivory teeth, how deep
The garnet red of your taxidermized tongue.*

With the knife, he dives to extract a succulent ball
From the sleeping root, each potato a dream
Unmindful of its own largess, fat as a small, fat man.

II

The she-bear walks sideways, pretending
Not to see the shadowed space of open being
Before her—morning, an unsuspecting rabbit.

Noon, an alarmed, slippery weasel. Evening,
The ox a tribe of mendicants had lain on an altar
Before slitting its throat to God. The frightened larynx

Is a secret roar ringing between the fingers of dawn,
Waking the fat man from sleep like a potato
Pulled from its moist bed in the earth. Again

He takes up the she-bear's brute burden, woman now—
Heavy hips, pendulum breasts, an indigo voice—
Bringing all his organs into awareness of peripheral

Movement—a throat opening and ending on the desire
Of one bullet—balanced on the fulcrum of sacrifice
And animal intention that won't quiet or wait.

III

Love is a hot, buttery potato melting on the tongue
Of the fat man, the fur rug still singing a forest song
Against his buttocks. Love makes a miracle of pain,

Dream-work in sleep, peace-work come dawn.
Love appears in the fat man's skin shining above
The promise and pull of muscle and flesh,

In the immaculate hide of the she-bear cured
To keep accomplishment and comfort intact.
Love appears in the eyes and smiles of those

The fat man greets on the street, in his first breath
Upon waking, in the blood captured inside the body,
In all that heaves, in everything white, everything brown,

Everything green. Love is not in a clock, or anywhere
Fear reigns. Triumph over potatoes may be love.
Triumph over animals is not. Every she-bear gets her due.

IV

There is ice on the window when the fat man wakes
From his buttery-fur sleep. Each potato has become
A temple in his once empty stomach housing

A fat woman, a she-bear. A starling calls like an alarm,
The mourning dove answers only after his beloved calls.
Dawn spreads a pink skirt over the horizon, exposing

Large, rosy thighs and the wonder of a magenta belly.
Then, a memory the fat man held close as a thin child—
The linden tree rising grand outside frost-filigreed glass

Holding a nightingale in its branches, the same bird
That called him forward in the forest to meet the body
Of the bear. They are both older and more round now,

Connected by hunger and sinew, just as the ligament marries
Flesh to bone around the joint that swings the whole body
Free, once it has met its match and mate, and gotten meat.

The Altar

For sure, the brain is a fool. The Priest of Hope
Has abandoned the Temple of Gray Matter,
Seeking the sweeter climate of Assyrian-blue.

What's left in the bare hollow? A high-vaulted ceiling
And stone floor, devoid of worshippers.
The alter—home for a spider. *It's nothing,* you think.

But then, there is the spider. There is a new, elaborate web.
Grief, the interim minister, preaches eight ways
Of forgetting—intellect and abandon, health and debauchery,

Exertion and lassitude, desire and disdain. The heart
Keeps beating beyond what's been lost by the delightful,
Singular body you've been gifted this time round.

About the Author

Susan Whitmore is the author of four poetry collections: *Your House is Floating* (Liquid Light Press 2013), *The Melinda Poems* (Pudding House Press 2004), *The Invisible Woman* (Singular Speech Press 1991) and *The Sacrifices* (Mellen Poetry Press 1990). Whitmore has a BA from Vassar and an MFA from Emerson. She taught creative writing and literature at the University of Nebraska—Lincoln and the University of Missouri Kansas City.

www.ingramcontent.com/pod-product-compliance
Lightning Source LLC
Chambersburg PA
CBHW021025090426
42738CB00007B/911